PRAISE FOR

The Erotic Papyrus

"Sonja the power of your knowing speaks volumes, your wisdom is deep and abiding, imbued with love, a nectar my soul indulges, and I am nourished. Poets speak a sacred dialect, few understand, it emanates from the depths of the soul reserved for the Gods and Goddesses, which, of course you are. May others enjoy your wisdom and charm, as much as I do. Thank you!"

—Vibhuti Srimatadas

"Sonja, you inspire that which is good and perfect in us all. Your words call upon the beauty of love, love and the sanctions of the heart—Words that inspire the romantic, and give rise to the thoughts of passion—you are truly a gifted poet....Your mastery of seduction through word and thought is conveyed in each of your well inspired verses. Your world has garnered a captivated audience that continues to grow. We all admire you as you inspire our inner thoughts....Time has only enhanced what has always been, with the passing of each season, you have become more and more beautiful than the one before. You, dear Goddess, are the epitome of grace, beauty, and sensuality."

—Richard Briggs

"Let the Goddess Sonja connect with your kundalini energy with her unique and sensual writing style! Her words stimulate both the root and third eye chakras as her words take your mind deep to its pleasure centers. She has a way of allowing your mind to release its inhibitions and she guides you on an erotic yet sensual journey! Each poem is just one of many perspectives we all encounter. It's as though she recounts past life love experiences that connect with you so deeply, your brain releases oxytocin and endorphins as her words take you on a spiritually sexual pilgrimage to your inner most desires. As she lures you into her corridors there's no return; release and enjoy as your learn about yourself in her writings!"

—André D. Henderson, Advanced iNERGIES LLC

"Sonja, I love your poetry. Your knowledge is a gift that many of us have, but choose not to embrace . The school's of thought are open, but only the gifted will war on to the next realms. You have always had that spirit of truth. Ask me how I know."

—Alex Harper

The Erotic Papyrus

GOLDEN DRAGONFLY PRESS

2017

Erotic Papyrus

Return of the GODDESS

Sonja Phillips-Hollie

CONTENTS

I dedicate this book to all the women in the world. Sharing with them the knowing of their past struggles, giving them a new found Breath of Goddess, whispering their names, supported by the collective. Our world now depends on us, to rise, and support this divine feminine energy, so we may come to see the power of Goddesses Uniting.

I also would like to dedicate this book to all of my readers who follow my poetry and to all of those who have encouraged me to write.

Introduction

From the high priestess of erotic poetry...
It was written long ago.

Her presence stirring in your soul. Even
before you see her...the goddess returns from
the otherworldly realm with a passion that
can no longer be hidden from the world.

Her words say many things, with numerous
connotations even for and to the uninitiated,
words that carry life, immortalized on papyrus,
casting a spirit of ancient knowledge.

Sexuality explored through the erotic mind
of the creator goddess. The goddess brings her
sexuality spiced with essence of ancient secrets.
She gathered through time and space.

Goddess has returned—

Experience the eroticism of Sonja Phillips-Hollie.

Goddess of the Nile

The
Goddess
is
Emerging
Body
Wet,
Drenched.
She
is
Surrendering
for your
erotic
pleasure.
Her
Lotus
erupting.
Hypnotizing,
even
the
gods.

Enter My Realm

Close your eyes
As I gently enter
the portals of your mind.
Taste my lust
Feel my surges
Embrace the darkness
Follow me to the other side
Where fantasies are made
Where nothing is sin
And nothing is denied.

Sacred Lotus

In the darkness of night
Her love calls out to me
From the past.
A sacred energy,
burns inside of me.
As we lie down
Together
with destiny
The sacred lotus
opens her ethereal petals.
Surrendering her soul eternally
With nectar abundantly
Drenching the roots of our sacred tree.
Our love is
That single point of infinity,
In which galaxies are formed
Civilizations arc born
And the universe is adorned
With our divinity.

Sculpted by the Gods

A silhouette of love
Perfected
In god's own art
Christened,
in the purest divinity
Infused as one
In an ocean of liquid dreams.

Daughter of Isis

Out of the darkness
I have arisen
From a galaxy of thoughts.
The Immanent One
As you enter
The temple of the gods
I am the sacred heavens
The Daughter of Isis
From my birth
Throughout the eternities
All that I am
I have created.

Sacred Temple

I am the sacred temple—
Where spirit and flesh
Unite.
As hidden truths
Uncover the darkness
I am led into the
Prevailing light.
It is here,
Where love reaches
Deep inside of me—
Down into the innermost
Parts of me
That often remain
Hidden,
From the
rest of the world.
It is here
Where I become nature
And nature becomes me.
Within my sacred temple—
Beyond the myths
And delusions.
I begin to see reality.
As I return to love
Love embraces me.

Ancient Hymns of Her

She is awakening to the songs of her inner goddess.
She is learning to dance in her own darkness.
She is chanting a new song, daring to be different.
Beneath the quieted moon, undisturbed
Lost in the ancient hymns of her.
I hear a voice that is mine, and another.
A timeless rhythm, within the depths of my soul.
I came to know her.
We are one in nature.
Her, the other within.
She has taken me to a place of solace.
The deep inner knowing that lives within me
I wish never to return,
Reclaiming the power once held by her.
Her divine light is emerging.
The goddess has returned.
From her lips to my heart
Her best intentions are kindled by something
more than flesh can touch,
More than words can obtain,
She is lifting us into the highest forms of love.
She is wounded but loves so deeply.
Estranged from the gods, her love diminishes not.
She sings on, resurrecting the Eden within herself.
I hear the song of a goddess.

Aligning with the inner rhythms of nature
Aligning with the soft anthems of the sky.
I can hear the musical intonations of the universe in
        her being.
Her enchanting music uniting the inner and outer realms.
Beneath the quieted moon, undisturbed
A universal song of love.
Lost in the ancient hymns of her.
My inward journey is just a wandering home.

The Goddess and I

Seducing me into her mystical world.
Forgotten passions ignite
She has set my soul on fire.
Kissing me gently with her truth.
Her body aglow.
As we lie beneath the stars
Staring into her eyes.
I see a glimpse of heaven.
Our souls unite.
We become as one.
The Goddess and I
Creating multiple worlds
Both of us knowing
that once her sacred wings unfold,
there is no turning back.

Erotic Papyrus

She has returned from the other worldly realm,
with a passion that can no longer be hidden from
      the world.
Before you see her, you will feel her presence
      stirring in your soul.
Her words say many things, with numerous
      connotations
even for the uninitiated, words that carry life,
immortalized on papyrus, casting a spirit of
      ancient knowing
from the priestess of erotic poetry.
She comes in her silky white gown through the
      mist of time.
Ready to explore your eroticism deal with your lust.
As the sacred heavens open
She lures you into her corridors of no return.

Awaken to the Sun

Awaken to the Sun
It is the light outside
Of myself,
Black dust
Like ashes arises,
In this world
I am bound
Like angels falling,
Soulless and unknowing.
Bathed in delusions
Intoxicated with sin
Resurrected
Into this matrix
That never ends.
Out of darkness
Beyond the stars
My soul awakens.
Unto the Sun,
Which nourishes,
Protects
And guides me
To the other side.
On this journey

I am traveling,
In and out
Of portals,
Entering into
New dimensions,
Hidden
So deep inside
The eternal covenant
Of my mind.

Immortal Love

A beautiful journey,
that you were on.
What you have brought
back is pure love.
You shall remember
more in the next lifetime.
The others
will not understand
what you mean.
But I will...
I want you in the light,
As well as in the dark.
What is cryptic to them.
Will be evident for us.
Entombed in your words
Our fate is sealed.

Beyond the Veil

Appealing to the eye seductive in word.
Many have become addicted to her as their fantasy.
Mortal eyes covet that which the soul conceals.
Her beauty only camouflages what lies beneath
      the surface.
Exiting the sarcophagus of self.
She unlocks other worlds.
The untouched part of her.
Separating the veil between heaven and earth.
Transported from Eden
Her only sin is in the knowing.
The becoming is the unbecoming of me.
The Poet and the Goddess.
They are one.
Lifting the veil.
Her kingdom of vanity crumbles.
Slain by the truth of her own perceptions.
A sacred metamorphosis.
In the dual nature of one's soul.
Are the gods masquerading as us?
Half tithing in her sorrows.
Love unveils.
In a world of solace.
She awakens to her greatness.

Awakening of Lily

Beauty blossoms so perfectly
Delicate in every way
A flower spun
In alluring simplicity
Lily is her name
Passions purest love
Admiring her nakedness
Adorned in a white silhouette
Untouched by imperfections
Binding our sacredness
In a lasting solace
Whispers an unforgettable love
That touches inward
Awakening a new form of you.

Inner Poet

There is an
inner poet inside of me,
She won't let me be
Now that she has awakened,
I don't think she'll ever go back to sleep.
On most lonely days
I searched for her
[reaching inside of her only to find me]
Like a ghost sitting beside of myself
She is always there
[that part of me no one else can see]
My unspoken prayers,
My beginnings and my ends,
An angel soothing my demons
Soaring on heavenly winged words—
To places within.
Lurking in the mystical winds,
Both of us swept away
By lavender scented dreams…
Where the magic of poetry is born.
As my spirit awakens,
Her words bloom
Into petals, prose, and stems—
Sprouting from my lips,
Created from love's depths
So that our gifts
May someday flower
humanity.

Imprints of You

Your imprint is within my heart and your energy
is within my soul. I am a haven for your joys, your
sorrows, your yesterdays and your tomorrows—
and yet it is the here and now that has embraced
you with the essence of my being. I not only love
you for who you are
but for who we have always been together.

Wings of Sovereignty

I stood out on the edge of
Somewhere and nowhere
Beyond the wings of sovereignty.
A goddess hidden so well
No secrets beyond self.
As the raven
Abandons the dove;
I emerge from the darkness
A stigmata of love.

A Desert Rose

A desert rose in need of rain
Her body gripping my every word
Exiled in a mirage of thoughts.
Quenched by her endless waters
Time and love suffused
Blowing sand kisses in the dunes
Her body dissolving into mine
Many lifetimes ago
We created Eden,
while I held her
Love pardoned all sins.

Beauty of Isis

Shadows of the clouds
The sun cloaks
Giving balance to the beauty of my flesh
I recognize the language of the trees
Being harassed by the wind
It whispers to me
Regarding my lust for Isis
My loins suffer,
My heart beats stronger
My spirit ravishes Isis
All over her body with my lips
Drenched in wine of the gods
Even her shadow makes me lust
Until the sun returns
The moon gazes at her
In the shadows of the clouds
Her beauty never fades
Making the skin that holds
The beauty of Isis
The trees tell me to protect and cherish
The lust of my loins
Until the afterlife
We will be
Satisfied.

Holy Essence

I am the holy essence.
hidden inside the deepest corner
of your mind.
A love that lives inside of you
A burning lust,
Never consummated.
Breathe my air
Feel my love
I am the light
When there is no sun
I am the eternal fountain
Pouring out lustful indulgences
Without me, there is no surge
As you go deeper
My Lord,
Deeper
Dive into its presence
Open the sacred entrance
To my inner heavens.

Inner Beauty

There is such a peaceful beauty at her outer core
But it only camouflages what is within.
It appears your beauty only camouflages what
Lies beneath the surface.
You seem to radiate so much love,
Yet so few give you the love you deserve.
Most that pursue you
Only pursue your beauty in lust
rather than the truth portrayed in your words.
Were they but to see the real you
The loneliness of a soul
Wandering endlessly—
She is in search of that one true love
that is able to capture all of you, mind, body and soul.

Isle of the Gods

On the Isle of the gods
Her passion flows
Like an endless river
back and forth.
As the tides
Meet and mingle.
Her wetness is
Betrothed to his form.
As the heavens open
He enters
She enjoys
He is pleased
As they become one.

Sols Kisses

Blown in glass Sols kisses,
Caught in your hair a fragrant lemon fire,
The epoch and departure of love
Haunted by your touches.
As shadows fornicate the dusk,
With each passing night,
Spent with thee,
I shall mourn the sun.

Infinite Skies

Journeyed my soul
Into the infinite skies
Where dreams are born
Amid the magical stars
Forever and ever;
My love is entwined
In moments of nostalgia.

Sharing the Sun

Sharing the same space
With the sun
But we are not harmed,
Because our bodies have evolved
into a different substance.
An Eternal flame
Within the depths of my soul
We have always been.

Flames of a Goddess

There is something about her rebelliousness
that turns me on.
She has a strange uniqueness
That I find very appealing and hot.
Singed by her undying love.
She has reached places inside of me
no one has reached.
She is the most captivating spirit.
I have ever encountered.
She dominates my thoughts incessantly
Even when we are apart.
I become so lost in her.
My soul has found its fire in her otherness.
I want, need and absolutely adore her.
Regardless of what we've been through
Our connection has grown deeper
And my love for her is a blaze.

Realm of the Goddess

As you enter my realm
You will fall deeply
Into the cosmic arms
Of a gentle goddess
Who wishes to connect
With your mind, body, and soul.
As she touches you
ever so magically.
Sprinkling her
Stardust
Of vibrant colors
All over you
Her mystical wings
Will carry you
On a sensual journey
Exploring every orb
And dimension.
As I devour all of your
Powerful essence
My soul thrives
Feeding off of yours.
Nevertheless,
In perfect harmony,
As my thoughts penetrate
your consciousness,
Your thoughts
Reside in mine.

Unveiling the Mystery

I am from somewhere.
I am from nowhere.
I am a stranger in a faraway land.
On a journey beyond self.
I am the love that cannot be unfelt.
I am the one of many.
Traveling through many places, and many lifetimes.
I am your unbridled thoughts.
I am the words that touch you deeply within.
Unveiling the mystery.
I am the ancient truths stirring in the winds.

Ðark Orchard

Inside the solemn verses
Of this forgotten poem.
My soul has taken refuge
In the purest of thoughts
Where love grows
A purple iris now blooms
In this dark orchard
Where death courts life.

A Rare Flower

Her colors are so many and so is her beauty.
She is soft.
She flows free but yet planted firm
She rises above to spread her joy
As the sun , moon, and rain
Even day or night
Have their way with her.
Her nectar is sweet
Even the bees want a sip or taste
Of her beauty.
From out of nowhere she came
And now that she is here
things are not the same
The orange, the red, the white and green
How can all be wrapped up into one?

Synchronicity

Confessions of love
Falling to their doom
Like mortal angels
Shrouded in mystery
Delicate in form
All of us different
And yet,
Inherently the same
Leaving lasting imprints
Wherever we lay
As time stands still
In awe of itself
A wonder of wonders
Disguised as a dream
Each pristine petal fading
Softly into nothingness
Clinging to their fate
Again and again
Covered in a wintry veil
of synchronicity.

Imitations of You

Night after night
Guilt was a guest
Masquerading as you
Inside her empty walls
It was your love,
I couldn't clone.

In the Rain

My body is trembling
Just imagining
You and I
Alone in the rain
This will be with me forever.
Dive into me
Delved into my imagination
The noise of the rain
The sounds of love
The silent longings
to hold you—
to kiss you ever so gently
all over your body.
To know you for myself.
Soon my love soon
Our time will come.

A Flower of Passion

Love possesses naught
A rose unpicked
Is a rose most sought.
In this sunless garden,
His love in winter
My love aches for yours.
A flower of passion
Pricked with thorns,
My heart bleeds
Where temptation blooms
My love grows.

A Ghosted Touch

Dark clouds
Run from the day
Instilled in the bedroom
Of night,
Forms of protested love.
There is no ending
In unions of fate
Just reoccurrences of what is
Ancients in-mixed
Of lust,
All that is ended in you.
In the silence of betrayal
The darkest love
brings a ghosted touch.

Mystic Eyes II

I can feel her mystic eyes penetrating me
Longing for my touch
Inviting me into her world
She knew exactly what I wanted
The sweet lure of her passion
Drawing me into her realm of pleasure
Like a wolf-tress fulfilling my licentious wants.
A stunning creation embossed in white
Oh, how the seductive nights cling to her
silky smooth skin
Heart of an angel
A body of a goddess
Lying half-naked as she poses for me
Staring at the contour of her body
Painting her into my thoughts and dreams.
My sacred lotus she blooms only for me
No longer empty
Erasing all her loneliness
Seeing beyond what is visible and into the heart of me
She is loving me so completely
That I carry her spirit inside of me always.

The Love Between

The love between two poets
Spills endlessly, from quill to quill
An unstoppable force;
Like an ocean with no depth.

Portrait of Love

Soft imaginings of her
Fill my lonely nights
As sensual poses of her
Captured in paintings,
Obsessively haunt me
As they hang
On my decaying walls.
I sit and stare into this lifeless
Portrait of her.
My soul becomes restless
As my eyes peer
At the soft pink rose petals
Adorning her naked body
The beautiful images of her
Still inhabit my mind.
She was the sweetest wine
I have never tasted
Drunk with insatiable desires
My weary heart pangs
Incessantly for the one
I love the most
I shall never have
Nor, ever know
I am left but with only
A quaint memory of her
Immortalized on the walls
Of my heart.

Infinity

Infinity held me
Beyond the imperfections of who I am
Beyond the loneliness and pain
Where only pure love exists
Soaring like a dove.
Her tears unnoticed
She came and went
A dreamer of dreams.
Searching and longing
For that which has never left.

Erotic Moon

The moon taunts the dark
Lasting imprints of her
Often distorted.

Sisters of Infinity

My inner glory.
I have beheld.
The infinite unbodied,
bodied in flesh.
She who came before me.
Adorned as goddess.
Hidden in the dark corridors
of my mind.
We are one breath,
Shared
through the vortex
of one soul.
Manifesting as love.
Arousing fiction
only the winds can provoke.

Love Reaches In

Love reaches into me
Reaches all the way in
Into the deepest part of me
Lifting the veil
Evicting the darkness
Shattering my world
Bringing me into myself
Into the divinity
That dwells in me
That often remains
hidden from the world.

Gazing into Your Eyes

Gazing into your eyes
I see your desires
The longings of love
The moments painted of us,
And the passions—
You felt so deeply
After my words
Brush against you softly
The heavens whispered
"We don't have to rush"
Thoughts of you running
through my mind
Dreaming of Autumn
Her corals unfold
The thoughts you held
The moments you enter
I see it in your eyes
All the beautiful moments
When you're alone with me.

Freedom's Song

As the night
Begins to slip away
Our spirits gathered
At the river
Our minds—
have yet to cross.
Shackled by
Our own thoughts
Our souls exiled
In black lands
disinherited
Beneath
A vigilant moon
Freedom's song
Unsung.

Black Isis

You are the progenitor of all races.
all begins and ends with you.
born of dark matter,
sunlight frozen by time compressed
and spoken into being,
as is the black diamond,
light is in you,
not a reflection of you!

Defiance

In this dark attic
She hangs
Forgotten and entombed.
A young slave girl.
Dressed in plantation white.
Her daunting eyes
Staring back at me
Our souls died,
yesterday
Like ghosts we fled
Into the night
Defiant against the winds
Her journey became mine
As I inherited her dreams
I can still hear her screams
That dreaded night
If only love had wings
I would set her free
A part of me wishes
To cut her down
From this rope
That binds her body
Not her spirit
A silence to a closing
As our souls merged
She was my past
I, her future.

Drums of Anticipation

I hear the beat of Africa's drums
And her drums are beating the loudest
As she calls out to me
from the land of the gods
My anticipation grows stronger
I can feel her heart pounding inside of mine.
As our bodies move to the same beat
the ancient winds cradle us
In this moment, we are one
the divine precession of the sun
reaches its peak.

Black Rain

On the edge of despair
Lust shivers down her spine
She was an offering
Naked—Simply divine
She was wet
in all the right places.
Raised her hips
Drove me insane
Love engulfed me
Her sultry words
Pouring into my soul
Like black rain.

Storms of Love

The storms of love
Enraged by truth
Holding on to fading illusions
Her kingdom of vanity crumbles
In the solitude of her tears
Begat the tearing down of her walls
She tames her darkness
As the divine
Inscribes…
Love upon her heart
The two become one
her soul takes flight!

Letters in the Sand

Sand is tiny letters to you
Each a promise to run
Against winds that heaven forms.
Time and love fissured
in pressure, glass
Is inevitable as is
my unbreakable love; [It is]
as if love had grown wings
Soaring into the untouched skies
Your thoughts reaching into mine
Like a flirtatious breeze
Our souls forever connected
Across the oceans
Endless as time.

Strands of Jasmine

Under skies of promise
Her wishes fly
Into the gentle breeze
Filled with scented dreams
bathed in jasmine.
A satin doll
with silver wings
Blooms in the garden
of our hearts.
Sown from
the ancient soil of love.
her beauty remains
hidden in the strands
of jasmine.

Autumn's Love

I am the fragrance of love,
lingering on the subtle breeze.
Bringing seeds
from the wilted flowers,
That will bloom once more in the Spring.
In this world we have created,
My lover and I dwell
Within the pages of yesterdays journal.
There are clichés; so many words
Linking us forever,
to yesterdays memories
revealing themselves as,
forgotten verses of my poetry.
We are a tale of lost love
The kind that tugs at someone's heart.
That little bit of me you will someday crave
The lust, the lingering the waiting within
can only be caressed by the stroke of a pen.
As today departs and becomes tomorrow
I bid farewell, to the part of you,
That dwells in me.
I should have moved on long ago,
Run from the pain.
Long before I became addicted to you.
In the silence of Autumn's love

I remember when at the stroke of the pen
There were dreams I could possess.
Though you locked her away in
Yesterday treasure chest.
Today, I am releasing the Goddess.

Where the Angels Fly

We have silenced ourselves so much
until we have become the silence.
Where the angels fly
Into the nothingness of everything.
The mind of god lives in the innocence of the child.
Far away from the darkness, rocking us to sleep.
For those hurts that impel us to turn to fantasy.
Even the sun fled beyond the moon.
Here where truth is untold;
We must seal the doors where evil dwells.
My restless spirit answering the call
of my soul.
No longer chasing ghosts in blue skies.
My wings exhausted
I sat down to write this poem.
For all the innocent children
I had to learn that I couldn't save everyone.
I had to love beyond fear.
Even the wind has eyes, now that you've seen
there is no unseeing.
This knowing shall forever be mine.
The invisible becoming the visible.
The divine child awakens
Helping us remember a world—

that we used to know.
We cannot remain silent.
We are the light born of darkness
What we think,
We unknowingly become.

White Roses of Tomorrow

I give you white roses
In remembrance of me.
My sweet child of August.
Symbols of love
Never to part from thee…
Stones of Peridot
Cherished eyes of grey
A daughter so precious
Guardian angels,
Watching over you,
I do pray.
Autumn winds blow
Reminders of that day
You gave my life meaning
In the comfort of my arms
You did lay.
Joys of motherhood
Erasing days of sorrows
Holding on to yesterdays
with white roses
of tomorrow.

Life is a Journey

There are so many of us rushing
As we run to catch the train.
We are rushing to get nowhere.
Life just keeps on passing us by.
Lonely among so many people.
Some of us have stopped living while living.
People come
People go
A constant stream
Never stopping to smell the roses
Or wave at the elderly couple
we just pass by.
Did you even noticed the little girl
twirling her red umbrella in the rain?
I guess we are just too busy.
Running to catch that train.
carrying suitcases
filled with empty promises,
 expectations and dreams.
Life is a journey
You will shed many versions of you
On your path to peaceful love
It can be so magical and beautiful.
On a voyage inside myself
I have lived so many lives

Traveling through time
so many unexpected places
I went through all the people
I've loved in my life,
and all the trains
we have had to take,
all the paths,
we have had to cross.

Love Awaits

A lustful flower
In your gown of midnight
blowing in the subtle winds
leaving me breathless with desire
As I watch you lose yourself
in love and lust
under the pale silver moon
Watching you
become multiple goddesses
Tossing and turning.
I have lost my mind chasing after you.
All the nights we could've been together
But the darkness conflicting with the light.
When love seems to go wrong
We build cathedrals to console
our pain
Haunted by the lover I never let in
You are the secret,
I must never share
the magic of the newness
that it brings
Touching all
the untouched rooms
inside of me.
In the absence of your fire.
My sheets burn.
Cast thy canopy
The morning comes soon.

Apparition of Love

A nostalgic longing
For that which was lost
On a mystical path
Love defies time
As a gorgeous apparition
in vintage white.
I find consolation
in the sonnets of love
etched inside of my heart
by a phantom
I once loved.

Apparition of Love II

Love Is
A gorgeous apparition
Leaving herself inside of you
Wherever you may go
Unleashing,
her mystical powers
Leaving your soul
Naked and unguarded.

Inseparable

I shall
Love you in silence
Until the day,
I die
You are
An inseparable part
Of who I am.
One soul
Drawn to the same light.
It is impossible
To sever you
From my world.

Twin Flames

I will feed your mind
Which will feed your body
And soul
With a fierce energy;
A love so intense
Some have fallen in love
Without even touching me.
As my love delivers
Powerful downloads
Deep impulses shall
Surge in and out of you
Igniting twin flames!

My Lilith Fair

She's who she is to the world
But she is who she is with me
When the world is not there
She is unseen but felt
She loves me
And her love means the world to me.
Her flower
Is my flower
Her most precious everything is mine
And mine, hers
My Lily
My Lilith Fair
My love
My world when the world is not there.

Song of Eternity

She played a song for me.
A different kind of song.
A song without words.
A song of eternity.
A song that only I could hear.
A soft melody of love delicately woven
from each of my heartbeats.
I am falling in love with her all over again.
As we journeyed into multiple worlds.
Each night a different dimension.
Exploring the unknown,
the untold and the mystical.
Lost in the momentum of a goddess.
Lost in the rhythms of love.
Lost in her for all eternity.
Only she could hear the song…
playing in my heart.

Yesterday's Arms

I cling to him
As if it were you
Fate slips between
two worlds
Reaching for tomorrow
Love held me
in yesterday's arms.

Rapture of Love

I gave you that part of me
That always belonged to you
That part of me only you understood
In a place where only you and I exist
Hidden within my sorrows
We are parts of the same pieces
Enshrouded in love
As black tears poured
From your soul
They fell from my eyes
Mending my soul
Breaking through
All of my barriers
No one has ever found
That part of me
That fits inside of you
So perfectly.

Deeply Within

A ghostly vision of her
Lingers on the shores
She comes and goes
In guises naked
Erecting my world
Love speaks for itself
Deep within
The ocean of my soul
Like a sea goddess
Silver in waters
Galore—
My reality is hers
Not a mythical lore.

Unloyal the Nights

Unloyal the nights
Beneath a sinister moon
She covets my soul.

Until She Returns

Into the quiet of winter, my thoughts wander
Blending in with the colors of life
Love is finding herself wherever she longs
as if trying to attract and distraction
nature flaunts her beauty
by painting the world inside outside of us
reminding us of how precious life truly is,
innocently given,
yet beautiful in its own way
She manifests in myriads of forms.
Until she returns,
a lil bird [as if god]…perched
on a wintry branch, admiring itself in all.

Forbidden Realms

Fate summons her lover
Into the mystical realms
Distance avails not
As the white fog
Covers her intentions
A new sin she awoke
Sinking into flesh and spirit
Bridging the emptiness of life.

Sea of Love

Drifting in a sea of love
Flooding my soul
Like an endless oasis
His mystical tongue
Creating swirls of energy
Around my exquisite pearl
As we fully indulge
I am at his mercy
As he explores my chambers
And forbidden cove
In this sea of love
We are both drowning
To become as one.

The Muse

Mysterious is love
When words are not
Befitting to the touch,
As she hears
"I love you"
So much.
Succumbing to the darkness
She moves impetuously
Into love,
She clings
To the power of love
To release her,
But she is his muse.

Within Me

I lie awake
Lost in my thoughts
Overwhelmed with desire…
Overflowing with love
A woman's heart
Is an unstoppable force
Her mind
A strange and mystical place
A holy sanctuary within me
Shielding me from all pain
Covered in her own glory
Her eyes as distant
As the sky
As bright as the stars…
Drawing you into soft
Clouds of compassion
As it covered her soul
with a blanket,
destined for a dark
journey.

A Place Called Desire

I arrived at our place called Desire only to find
    the cabin empty
Looking out the window the bright moonlight
Allowed me to see you cooling in the fresh water
    of the pond
I stood there watching you as you slowly began to
    emerge from the water
The light of the moon glistening from the moonlight.
As you walked to the place where we sat under
    the tree
reflecting on the beauty of this place that is ours alone.

Everything for Eve

He is more than just a visitor
He dwells within her mind
He was the forever that lasts all night
His world is her solace
His wings her only consolation
His love her darkest sin
He is everything for Eve.

My Escape

I followed her into this place
I can't describe with words
A place that I wish
Never to return from
Lost in the abyss
Of impure thoughts
With every stroke
Blending into her world
Dark and sensual
The place of my escape
At the stroke of midnight
Volatile our love
As the desire for more
Shattered my world.

The Huntress and The Prey

She is both Huntress and Prey
She is always aware of her surroundings
And is prepared for the unexpected.
She is always in her element
Seeking her next opportunity
She blends into the environment so well
That she is seen only when she want to be seen
Sleek, sexy, and deadly
A body sculpted by the gods
When you think that you have her cornered,
You're already her trophy
She is a warrior when she has to be...
A Goddess at her essence!

Contemplating Your Touch

Contemplating your touch
And the indescribable feeling
I get as your fingers
Barely touch my delicate skin
Your tongue slowly gliding down
Just below my navel
The sheer anticipation of you
Removing my laced panties
And revealing my sacred flower
Is sending surges
Throughout my entire body
Allowing you to indulge fully
In my sacred gardens
Tasting my sweet juices
Building up your anticipation…
to enter my heavens.

Splashes of Me

A kaleidoscope of colors
ravishes my body.
A gush of summer
Springs forth
Unleashing
The Autumnal beauty
Inside of me.

Ocean of Bliss

I was the sun in an ocean of her love.
You were never in want or need.
You were a poet that made love to me through words,
creating an ocean of warmth inside of me.

The Huntress

The seductive night clings to her body
Covered in the darkest intentions
A Huntress disguised beneath a sinister moon
Dominion is hers,
She roams wild and free
All the wolves delight in her primordial beauty
Enticing her prey with the sweet lure of her passions
She instinctively draws them into her clutches
like helpless victims to be devoured whole.

Unthinkable

Last night,
He wrote the story of love
All over my entire body
Gently caressing my soul.
Like a novel with no ending
Inviting me into the darkest corners
of his mind
Filling up the empty pages of my heart.
Line after line
His thoughts held me hostage
with every stroke of his pen
He erased all of my inhibitions.
Inside of this story
I was his perfect ending
As we explored the unthinkable
He didn't disappoint.

Devour Me

As he undresses me
He undresses my love
Caressing my soul
where only he can
Naked before god
Heaven ignites hell
Her yawning abyss
Devours him from within.
Pulling her closer
Skin to skin
Into his eternity
For a lifetime of sin.

Unopened Gift

As the tempestuous moon
serenades my soul
with her delicate incantations
I can no longer refrain
Each night I return
peering through her window
behind the long sheer curtains
there lying on the bed
an unopened gift.
The sweetest temptation
staring back at me.
I was dying to open it.
This gift of love
wrapped in a gentle seduction
A silhouette of pink bows
caressing her soft back.
As I approach her chambers
I fall deeper into her clutches
longing to kiss
the slain parts of her
And to taste
the agony of my awaiting
haunting desires spilling out of me
unable to escape this fantasy
I close the door to this intangible dream.
For, lust has enslaved me
As each night I return to her.

Fruit of the Gods

I cannot see you hunger and thirst
for poetry so starved.
Share my lord with me
half of thy joys and sorrows.
In Nod, [paradise]
allow me to quench thy hunger
and ache for thee...
I am the sacred fruit of the gods
in which you so adamantly seek.

Dark Orchard II

In the dark orchard
l shall remain
A servant of love
As the night covers me
with her kisses of sin.
the moon hides
in the subtle realms
of sensual joining—
The stains of breathing
Lost upon me helpless
To all...
life and death
lie down as lovers.

Dark Orchard III

In her dark orchard love has bloomed
Her body aglow, singed to the core like the flames
    of Isis
His sinews taut and swollen as he ventures in
    pure bliss
Such a divine fragrance with a secret sense of
    seduction.
There her next victim enters her inhaled by her
    suction.
As she enslaves and binds him in fetters
Her blouse waiting to be singed with his touch
He opens his lowers and downs his shutters
A need for intimacy her hunger grows
As she offers he partakes, a sinful fruit grown to
    be eaten
Their bodies coiled like serpents as they lay
    motionless
But slow rhythm overtakes as he sees her back
    backless
Now their bodies entwined in the dark orchard,
    to be gods own.
His tongue impaling her sacred places as wind
    flutters her gown
She holds firmly as he probes deeper in her
    guarded palace
Her soft petals bloom and drip as his sinews seek
    solace.

Pristine Skies

Pristine will be the skies
when her morning spreads
As she stands in front
of the bare window
Awaiting her lover's return
The sun playfully caresses her skin
Softly inhaling the scent that she owns
Inviting me into her sinful thoughts
tempting a righteous falling
As lust stares into her window
leaving him at want for more.

Canvas of Love II

If I could paint love
I would paint her
Mystical soul and body
In many vivid colors
With a few strokes
Of dark seduction.
She would be
All that I could
Ever want
Or imagine.
A canvas
That would entice
My artistry,
As she'd be
My visual anomaly,
Immersed
In all the colors of her.
I'd use my phallus
As her brush
And paint
her insides plush,
Lathering her
With every thrust,
As we'd become one
On a canvas of lust.

Prodigal Daughter

You are
The prodigal daughter
A wayward angel
The universe is...
an extension of your soul
The whole world
Is overwhelmed with joy
To have you at the feast.
It needs your energy.

The Tents of Kedar

My body remains
as my spirit wanders
into the darkest tents of Kedar.
In search of my beloved.
Alone in my bed.
I begin to feel his surges
Like an arrow
Piercing through my heart.
A gorgeous apparition
I am his.
I am thy greatest craving,
thy darkest sin
Wandering
through the sand dunes
Every night, I hear his call
My love for him grows stronger
My pulse becomes his
bound to other worlds
We shall not rest
Until our souls
Merge as one
In the sacred tents of Kedar.

Sun-Kissed Wings

Eyes we closed in darkness
Opening to the light of dawn
The Mistress of my dreams
Lending her sun-kissed wings
Taking me into
her deepest oblivion
Fate has become
Her lover
Her reality
Her journeys end.

Feel Me

Feel me
Feel me in every moment.
Feel me in every way
Feel me when you're lying with her
More love, less judging
No apples here, just spirits
As my lips move up and down
We return to the garden of pleasures
Where the Tigris and Euphrates meet
No limits, No boundaries
As I transport you to Eden.
Where my words
Awaken and erect the gods.

Falcon Returns

Sleepless nights
Tossing and turning
Haunted by his memory
As whispers of our love
Echo throughout the halls
A falcon has landed
on my window seal
He brings everlasting comfort
I want so much to lie in his bestial wings
Forever
To feel his stronghold
Overtake me
In sensual foreplay
But our love is trapped
In the wrong dimension
My heart wept
Knowing one day
He must fly away
Never to return.
As our boundless thoughts
Formed intimacy,
He has left me one of his wings
He has taught me so much
But he never taught me
How to stop loving him.

Andromeda's Star

You can feel my gaze
I can feel your eyes
As they pierce through me
With the might of Andromeda's Star.
Illuminating me
With the magnificence of eternity
The silver thread of infinity.
The mother ship of humanity.
I have but one request
And that is to arrest the distance
Between Us
Oh, how I long to caress your face
Beyond the illusion of time and space
And dwell within the nucleus
From which our love shall never part.

Phantom of Love

I fell in love with a Phantom.
In my wake,
In my sleep.
He seduces me with sonnets of love.
Outside my window
Red roses,
He leaves to remind me
of our deepest infusions.
In my mirror,
His reflection lingers
Deep within the trenches of me.
Our love ignites
Forbidden passions.
Between mortal and immortal.
No saint in his soul.
I do not fear him.
Because I am the light to his dark,
His intentions are interwoven in me.
Suddenly, he appears,
Behind me,
Taking me into his arms.
I do not pull away
For he carries my souls out of its
darkest exile.

Thriving on my energy,
He seizes my body. I glance into his eyes
As his hands ascend up my silk gown.
He pauses,
To enjoy my satiable moans.
He claims my soul
As I call out his name,
In pleasure and pain.
My sweet requiem of blood
He must taste.
His gentle fangs drink of me.
I surrender
No saint in my soul.
We fade into the depths
of immortality.

Dark Novel

She couldn't help
lending herself
to the darkness
for just one night.
Obsessed, with the pages
of this dark novel.
She becomes drowsy
Falling into the story
Her lover emerges
His eyes
Pulling her into his world
She stares back into his
Leaving her world
Joining him forever in his.

Dark Novel II

His eyes
Pulling me
Deeper
And deeper
into the darkness
His touches
I crave
Soft moans
With no protests
I surrender to him
Where love bleeds
He tastes my needs
As he drinks
My sacred essence
I am now trapped
Inside the pages
Of his dark novel
Each
Page
Wanting
to be touched, felt, seen…
A dream within a dream
My soul
He has claimed
Impaled upon the altar
Enfolded in his dark wings.

Seraphs Wings

She was birthed
in a lovers moon,
A seraph of sifted wings
platinum in form
soaring impetuously
in between worlds.
A stunning creation
of attraction
Wings of silver
much higher than
sight or color
not hurt
with the hues of sin
fashioned in love.

The Sacred and The Self

In the sacred pairing of oneself.
The mystery begins—
where the destination ends.
The passion is separate from the love.
The love is sweet.
The passion is fierce and must be tempered.
Desires, our equal offspring.
Eternal and heartfelt.
Awakened here, only to forget
Each is eternal.

The Winds of Uncertainty

I can remember
as if it was yesterday.
A young bride
Lonely and isolated
The days turned into months
The months into years
I didn't know what the future held.
[It just wrote itself].
In your absence
Love had become a stranger
My precious children,
The only joy of my journey.
Dreaming of a better life
Releasing the pain
Never looking back
Leaving it all behind
In the winds of uncertainty
I grew wings of change.

Winter's Lust

In winter's lust for spring
Her petals exposed
Shadows of lust
Barren in the fall
of crushed leaves
Our souls rest suffused.

Sea of Deception

In the sea of deception
Love traps all
Flooding the heart
Like a surging current
I am swept away
By the beauty of words
Into the unknown
As the unknown
A mortal and her god
Hidden deeply within
A sea of ugly truths
And pretty lies
The storm subsides
The calm is her lover
Disguised as destiny
Herein is love.

Love Is

Love is
the fertile soul from which life springs forth.
Love is
the womb of original thought.
Love is
the place in which the gods walk back and forth.
Love is
the source that exists within us all
Love is
a value, which can't be bought
Love IS…

Love Held On

Into the vastness of the horizon
I soared on the wings of my thoughts
Chasing the same skies
Even after you have gone
Love has found her way back home
Purging me of myself
Calming the storm
Touching my soul
Where only you can
Hiding behind clouds of uncertainty
Barely out of darkness
I wanted it all
As long as it's with you
Even after, I let go
Love held on.

Ever After

She has fallen for a world
That she can never have
Enchanted by a love
She has never even felt
Holding on to a memory
Since she can't have the reality.
Lying in the arms of a fairytale
Wishing for an "Ever After"
That was never meant to be.

Enchanting Wings

Angelically mysterious
But godly formed
An image of perfection
Seducing us with
Her divine presence
In the moonlight
Her enchanting wings
Spliced to create love
Which is life
As she perceives it to be
On earth
As it is in heaven
Possessing the power
Over oneself
Long before souls
Had earthly bodies
They had wings.

The Perfect Storm

Darkened clouds above me
No turning back
Embracing the storms
My love expands
And becomes one
With all it sees and touches
For many years,
She has roamed
In this lower plane
Looking for her past love
Trapped between worlds
As the rain pours,
It leaves lasting imprints
upon her soul.
She becomes soaked
in thoughts of him.
Even when they are apart
They are connected
in a way that surpasses words.
Longing to avoid karma
And remain in his world
Our bodies
Marinating in liquid realizations
The storm has passed
She releases the pain
But not the love.

Inner Sanctum

I am not the same soul
I once was
For I have unmarried
Its yesterdays
And left its psalms of tomorrow
For the inner sanctum of today.

Love Offering

Lying upon the altar
I am dressed
In a long sheer gown
of pure white.
Offering the purest love
As impure thoughts
Invade my mind.
Awaiting my Lord
To consummate his bride.
Longing and deeply
Anticipating
Our sacred marriage
And the gentleness
He shall serve to me
As I surrender all to him
All my love
And sacred energy.

The Vineyard of the Gods

The night draws nigh
Luring me inside
The vineyard of the gods.
Sipping from her chalice
Of seductive thoughts
The taste of heaven
Is fruitful.
Yet intoxicating
Forbidden
Yet thirst quenching.
Dripping
With her essence.
The wine of the gods
Is bittersweet,
Yet I sip.

Heiress of Night

As the new moon awakens
I enter her dark chambers
The Heiress of night
She covets my soul
Where love never sleeps
Death hides
Like a ghost in the sheets
She came and went
Unforgettable, the nights
I lived in her fantasy

A Borrowed Love

What if I told you
Would you even listen?
That everything
He did to you
He did to me
All the romantic gestures
All the late night chats
The charming way
He made you feel
Oh, so special!
The promises that he made
But never kept.
Telling you
Telling me
That we should be discreet
Enjoy the love we shared
wishing and waiting
For him to be all yours.
What you should've seen
In his eyes but didn't.
I peeped his game
A long time ago.
The way he would
Turn his love off and on.

I kept my wall up
Knowing from the start
this love was crowded.
A love borrowed
never really belongs to us.
Alone and broken hearted.
Standing on the other side of truth
I may not understand
Your pain.
Or why you can't seem to let him go.
But, unlike you,
I loved me more!

Cleave Only to Her

Peering through mirrors of deception
Love sees what love is not
Seeming to have it all
But not having all of him
Dreaming of a love that would cleave only to her.
A beautiful gown, a reluctant bride
Unpacking all of his indiscretions
Never expecting him to bring along so much luggage.
Leaving his heart in so many different places
Deep down knowing she isn't the only one
Karma was just another one of his one of many
An angel of chastity, clinging to hope
Her light grows dim as love exposes the dark
The past taunts, tempts and even dances with her.

As I Am

You have created this image of me
This image of me that only you see
Instead of painting us together
You are captivated with exposing me
Look deeper my love
The eyes can deceive
I'm tired of explaining "Myself"
Everything I write
Is not always about me
You see what you want to see
Instead of what is really inside of me
You refused to see passed the superficiality
Sketching me into your world of insecurities
Molding me into your twisted perceptions
The goddess doesn't have the energy
To entertain this fantasy
A splash of me here
A splash of me there
Does not portray all of me
I feel this is more about you than me
You are not the only man that has been
Mesmerized by gods own art
If you are compelled to paint me
Then you must paint all of me
Mixing the good with the bad
Paint me as I am
I can only be me.

Andromeda II

Desires of mental stimulation rule my world
There is no need to roam any longer
Journey with me into the core of Andromeda.
Merging through portals of longevity
Stimulating your mind, body, and soul
The Goddess is ready to let you in
Knowing fully what to expect
You must go deep within my sarcophagus
Spreading my cosmic wings
Plunging deep into my forbidden realms
So that you can land your galactic ship
Precisely in between the temples of my ecstasy.

Embracing Love

In the arms of my beloved
I shall remain
Married to the moment
As time stands still
Our souls embrace
Pure and untainted
It is what the gods are made of.
I am daydreaming in my daydreams
He is giving me everything
I wanted
I needed
Yet, I feared
breaking down all of my walls
No beginning no end
Love is writing its own poem
His words reaching so deeply within
Touching my place of surrender
I am never letting go
of this Eden,
That we have created
You are the god to my goddess
I wish to give you all of me
The untouched part of me
Embrace my love
let me be your endless heaven.

Now and Forever

Our love is imprinted
Upon each other
And it will always be.
It takes no thought of
Time nor distance.
And there is no power
In existence
That can match its velocity.

The Creator of Worlds

A Creator of worlds
Her eternity was not long enough
He loved her before many worlds were formed.
Goddess and protector in the realm of the gods
Beautiful beyond all comparison
Sad and pained by her duties
She yearned for him too
Her Alpha Wolf
Her protector of worlds
She poured her heart out to him,
He held her like no other
They made love as only they could.
He had but one desire in all of the trillions of galaxies,
Her!

White Sand

As I lay naked in the white sand,
my restless heart longs to be somewhere else,
somewhere outside of this body where I can paint
my own skies provocative pink.
Listening to the seas as they crash
into the shore, my mind begins to wander,
Her ways a mystery of waves,
luring me into an unknown place.
Beyond the unsettled waters of my soul,
No longer adrift in inadequacy,
Emptying myself I dissolve in blue calm,
Gently pulled by the incoming tides,
I sink into the inner depths of being.
Engulfed in silence
Myself and Nature—
Her unbounding reach is love's purest form.
Reborn here, cleansed of mortal thought.
The Heavens color the inner shades of my being.
I return from the waves, come back to my shores,
soft sands surround the hushed gold of this place,
I rest in their ivory grace.
Nature sighs,
I have begun to feel divine touch.
I lay down beside love,
I surrender to god.
Drifting into the unknown,
crossing over to the other side.
Immersed in love.
Our bodies dissolve into one.

White Horse

She arouses a white horse but its imagination is
running away with a dream.
Uncloaked of mystery, inside of her naked thoughts.
Whispering her soul for flesh to penetrate the
pains within…intrigued by her,
A phantom on a white horse comes with a sword
and shield…
to tame her desires. Her mind screams for truth,
wandering in the unknown,
from a dream awakens emptiness, longing to
return to sleep to lick the desires of his
fingers. She follows him into the moonlight.
It is a slow death.
Falling into nothingness. Yet reaching the heavens.
We make love not as mortals, clothed in myths
but as gods.

Sacred Rings of Infinity

Let us make a pact with each other
At our last moment of breath on this earth
We will think of each other in the afterlife
if there is such a place.
And once we are reborn in another life.
We will remember each other and be together always.

Our pact has already been inscribed within our souls.
We will exchange the sacred rings of infinity,
and our bound to one another
as a heart is bound to the
expressions of Love and Passion.

We will make love as intricate facets of the universe,
at which time creation will explode
onto the canvas of the universe,
and our offspring will be the stars to guide seekers
back into the truth of their inner cosmos.
And I will caress your face,
kiss your lips,
and whisper with the voices
of a thousand raging seas…It is Good!

The Misty Fog

I am the shadow
hidden in the misty fog
with which you cover the sensual
nakedness of your restlessness
aching for a dark lover.

When We Ride

The gentleness of his hands between my thighs.
Has me trembling at the slightest touch.
As he caressing my soul.
Undressing my thoughts.
The moonlight is teasing me
Slipping in and out.
Quicken breaths and pounding hearts.
Just that one hand, can make me cum apart.

Secret Montage Within

Beyond this realm
Her secret chamber doth lie
In mutual passions
So enchanting, her eyes.
For some
Pleasures are begotten.
For others,
Desires never end.
Despised for her beauty within
Lust is the fruit
of an unforgiving sin
Uninhibited,
Our journey begins
Never to be released from this…
Secret montage within.

Waiting in the Shadows

You and I
Met
In the dark shadows
Of insidious lust.
Yet,
Beyond
the
shadows
Lies
Our infinite love.

The Rarest Jewel

A rare jewel
She has washed up on the shore
Desiring to be loved.
by the one who knows nothing of her world.
She longs for the right one to caress her soul
To kiss her where her clothes end.
To know her.
Set her free that is what she truly seeks
She is more than a mere beauty.
More than a body.
More than a few moments of pleasure.
She is a lady.
She is a goddess.
The ultimate gift to man.
The rarest of jewels.
Will her soul mate find her
before the tides of lost souls
washes her back out to sea?

Between Your Lines

I am squeezing between your lines, commas, and question marks. While choking on your pauses. You have taken my breath away. Your exclamations marks are so powerful. Your ink drips and drips. As I spray your walls poetically. I feel the touches of your words as I finger through your pages. They pass through the mind, and touch the soul and then the body. It is as if you know my deepest thoughts. I feel you in every line!

Held Only for You

How do I find the words to describe.
How much you really mean to me?
When words punish me with silence.
From a place no one else can enter
From a place deep within my heart.
I held only for you.
A love not bound by flesh.
A passion so deep.
Your love has moved mountains out of the way
to reach me.
Even on my most unflattering days.
You never forget to say, "I love you."

Irresistible

I am in love with love
All that she is to me
All that she does to me
I can feel her words
Purring inside of me.
I am in love with love
All that she has taught me
All that she has to offer
I am wet from her thoughts
Licking me gently.
Even when she is playful
She is irresistible.

Goddess You Are

You are the experience.
I always knew existed.
You are the words.
I long to hear.
You are the touch
I long to feel.
You are the breath I share.
You are the universe of love.
That I have always longed for
Goddess you are!

Sonnets of Love

Lost in the moment
Souls connected
Interconnected with verses of love
Written upon my heart like a novel with no ending
Embracing the me that had been hidden
His words awakening a love in me
that had been suppressed.
Penetrating
My mind
So deeply
Reaching inside of me
Piercing my soul
The deeper I drew him in
The weaker the walls became
The darker the thoughts
The greater my love for him
His words now caressing every bit of me softly
A secret desire no longer hidden inside of me
A great longing I held for him
Only for him
Peeking from its hiding place
His words piquing my curiosity
Filling me up with his sonnets of love.

Reflections of Me

Reflections,
Show her beauty
But not her deep longing for her prince.
Hidden within her distorted eyes
The ominous mirror projects not only
the darkness in her room
But foretells the uncertainty of his arrival
As the eerie night stares and taunts her
Will she ever find that one
who will kiss all of her wounds
Between the spiritual and the sensual.
As the shadows linger upon the unseen
walls of her mind.
She's caught in the web of his insatiable love
There is no escaping,
She concedes.

Sensual Pearls

Sensual pearls
Placed on smooth silky skin.
Lying on a black chaise
Naked and aroused
Gently touching herself
Destiny never looked so good.
Yearning for a sacred release
I crept inside of her world
Ripped her lace panties off
Tasting her sensual thoughts
My mind exploring
all her forbidden places
Amazed at my techniques
Her thighs tightened
and her body began to jerk
Uncontrollably!
Reaching its peak.
In that moment
I surrendered
letting go of my world
Erupting inside of hers.

Alluring in Red

A goddess appears in sensual red
Inviting me into her realm
Her body,
Soft and alluring
Her passions needing to be fed
Intimate thoughts of her
Lurking deep inside of me
She has an innocence about her
But her eyes beckon me.
Aggressive not passive,
Something about the color red
Brings out the bull in me.
She's a matador
Taunting my desire
I devour her innocence
Like the animal that I am, I attack!
Delivering thrust after thrust.
Giving pleasure to her
Beyond her expectations
No limits no boundaries
Tonight she wants nothing but lust
She just loved, all that I had to give
Dying for every inch of me
I take her to blissful ecstasy.

Affairs of the Heart

Never satisfied with just one
Whenever he traveled
He collected an assortment of flowers
Such a hypocrite
Showering them with all of his love.
Dripping with desire for her,
Her and her
Scribbling "I love you"
on all of their hearts.
He soon became careless
like a string of paper dolls
One by one
He cut out their hearts
using his wit and charm,
betraying all
that ever loved him.
Until his heart was left empty
Then She came along,
A heart that couldn't be tamed
To his dismay
Opting out of his foolish games.

Only Seventeen

Body of a Goddess
So innocent
Sweet and pure.
This divine lust from
Her youthful garden.
Has blossomed
into an exotic flower.
Her scent,
intoxicating the air.
She was only seventeen
Everybody wanting a taste.
She tried so hard
to keep the demons away.

Promiscuous

His love has caused a whirlwind
Everywhere the wind blows,
His lies blew…
Promiscuous like the winds
Seducing everything in its path
Blowing in all directions;
Caressing every flower
Neither here nor there
His love was everywhere.

Lust

I am Lord
In the house of lust
I am death and all its courts
Open thy mind
And receive me freely
And thirst not.
Lay in my walls
I shall cast out a beautiful mooring
You will catch my dreams
On the other side of the river Styx.
As your love sinks
Deeper and deeper
Into my forbidden realms
I will be your succubus
And swim in your lonely nights.

Craving You

I'm craving you
Craving me
Save me from this darkness
This silent obsession
Pull me out of my lust
Push your lust deep into me
Make this silent obsession
Scream your name
Take me
Make me yours
Oh My God
My God of love
Make me release
But never release me
I can't take it
How do your words make me
Do what they do?
I burn for you
Yearn for you
This spoken silent obsession
No longer able to be silent
Your words penetrating me
Invading my walls
Pulling thoughts through
Until lust has fled.

Kiss of Life

The irony of love and pain
Masquerading as lovers.
Dressed in a beautiful corpse.
Breathing in
asphyxiated air.
Gasping and choking me
With a kiss of life.

White Lingerie

White lingerie
Concealing—
Her dark intentions
Seducing me
Over and over again.
In her clutches
There is no escape.
Her body quivering
This long awaited night
Has come.
We have crossed the
Line of fantasy.
White lace panties
Slowly
being pulled down
Her honey coated thighs
Dying with anticipation
Her hidden realms
Lighting a fire
Deep within me.
Lying on my bed,
She slips into
My soul naked—
A sweet addiction
I long to indulge

Her in my sinful games
She feeds my deepest hungers
With the rush of white lace
Satin secrets
Dipped in soft pink persuasion.
She begs her lord
For endless thrusts
Of pleasures
That only he can give
As she moans to her god
In ecstasy—
He sprays her walls
With hieroglyphs
Her kitten PURRS!

Just Us

This love is perfect imperfect
It's us
What's for me is for me
And all of me for you
There's no erasing
The exclamation marks
scrawled down each other's backs
It all comes back
Recalled
With our names called
To the heavens and back
To this world within a world
No one can enter
Nothing can sever this love
Same longings
Same thoughts
They fuse us together
As one
Even apart
We are together
Merged
The other part of me
The other part of you
The other part of our souls that were missing
This belongs only to us
And we will always love each other more for that.

Trace My Lines

I ache to trace your lines
As my mind traces the lines
that connect you and I
Soft moans set the tone
Let us reach each other's souls
Let us be one with the love between us
Scream my name as I whisper yours
Until there is no trace of yesterday's echoes
Trace my lines
Let us read each other's souls
As my mind traces the lines that connect
You and I
Let us be one with the love between us
Until there is no trace of yesterday's echoes
Trace our unborn tomorrows
Our eminent destiny
Trace my lines
You will find some of you
In every one of them
Thoughts no longer separated
Trace the connection
That connects every bit of me to you
Reach my righteous
Teach me a love that might just...
Trace the lines that outline forever.

The Seductress

Inside of my wicked thoughts
My seductive angel awaits
Luring me into places unknown
Hot and sensual.
She is the ultimate aphrodisiac.
Her body sculpted by the gods.
I am so enchanted by her beauty.
I long to kiss her in places
Where dark is familiar
As she pulls my head deeper
Into her place of desire.
My sinful tongue probing
deeply within her delicateness.
Like darting snakes in a lovers duel.
Lips against lips
I lick the sweetness of her desire.
Her thighs trembling
With no hesitation-
I enter her garden of passion,
deflowering her place of joy.

Taste You

Taste you
I shall,
I do it so well
Licking so gently
The cream on top
Until the last drop.
I know you can't wait to see
What I have in store for thee.
As my lips erect monuments
You will say my name.
Before my fierce tongue
Swallows your midnights.

Be My Goddess

Tonight you will know the depths of my love. How much I want you. How I want to feel all of you. You will be mine. I will be yours. Claim me. Be my Goddess. I want you. I crave to be in you. I want to feel the goddess in you. The love that you have kept safe for me inside of you since the gods first roamed the earth. I know you want me as much as I want you. Feel now my sensual touches. As you enter my forbidden temple. Lose yourself completely. Give me all of you. As I have given myself to you. Feel now my deepest love. Grab my waist. Pull me into your world. Make me grab these white satin sheets. Take my righteousness. And when you feel my trust. Be my God!

Places Within

As I touch myself
I begin to think of you.
And all of the nights
You have been here before
Inside of my dreams
I feel your touches
When I touch myself
I draw aside the veil
in my temple of love.
I feel your lips—
gently kissing my navel,
and slowly moving downward
into the wetness
of my desires.
My soft wings begin to flutter.
I held my breath.
I was left numb and tingling.
As lust fled into the night!

Sensual Rains

Sensual rains pouring all over my body.
My nipples standing hard and erect.
Fantasizing about what you did to me last night.
Pinned up against that brick wall.
My thighs trembling.
As your hands slide underneath my skirt.
Exploring my desires
Your fingers probed my wetness.
My delicate peach throbbing.
As I ride your tongue...
all the way to erotic heaven.
Spreading my petals as you enter
My unguarded temple
Thrust after thrust
The feel of your thickness
My walls beginning to quiver
My body shaking uncontrollably
My flower erupts.
The rain sighs.
I cum for god!

Inseparable II

A Butterfly in November. I guess she enjoys her solitude. She never let too many people inside of her world. But, I could see behind her hard shell, into her softness. She almost always flew alone. She didn't let people get too close to her. The day she flew into my life. I couldn't wait to tag along. This shy and lonely butterfly. She helped out of the cocoon. Nothing could sever our friendship. Both of us soaring on wounded wings. It was like we had a golden thread holding us together. We were inseparable.

Love Unseen

It was love unseen,
Yet it felt more real
than a touch of flesh
It had no eyes
but beheld
the magnificence of her light
It had no ears
yet heard the musical intonations
of the universe within her being
It had no hands
yet, it wrote an unknown destiny—
and felt the vibration of her name
and it was "love"
not a love that is structured
and limited
by a carnal heart
but the love
which is responsible
for all that exists.

Eyes of a Goddess

In your eyes. I saw her, I didn't at first it took a moment. Studying every micro essence of your face. Every crevice felt familiar, I had tasted those juices, the sweetest in the universe. Your lips were the sun. My beloved goddess we have lived hundreds of thousands of years. Love, the pure energy that cannot die. You have silenced my storms with the...Forever in Your Eyes.

Away, I Fly

I could never be a part of someone else's love story...I deserve my own. I desire more than just your empty words...of nightly confessions leaked by your fictitious pen...unlike her, I let go. She kept forgiving you...until there was nothing left...the one you hold so dear oblivious to the one you claim to love, envious of the one you can't live without... when truth lies down with darkness...she uncovers a multitude of sins...so many roses in your garden, not enough love to go around...so many butterflies with broken wings. Away, I fly...I could never be caged...I must write my own story...a wise woman covered in her wounds...knows when love is real... love sets her spirit free.

A Mystifying Pull

How does one touch the untouchable
Even when one is mirrored in love
There is no escaping oneself
Pulling you deeper into the other world
How does one look the other way
How does one channel the spirit
into its proper place
When his love always catches her
before she falls
How does one not run when the night calls.

The Silence Awoke

Into the silence, I have fled. Betrothed to the unknown…no longer scripted by my own mortal thoughts…1 am barely here, just a ghost…lost in a fog of illusion…forever searching outside of myself…. wandering in the dark. Those who fell… sought not, that which exists within us all…behind the silvery clouds…love has kept me here…giving my thoughts wings. the night sang to me—until the silence awoke.

When It Rains

I will always think of you... when it rains... I can hear your heart beat... singing inside of mine... the sounds of the ocean... the calling of your name... the kisses of vanity... suspended in time... his and her bodies... enraptured as one... chastity lost in heavens abyss... love conquers all... there is no escaping her... endless bridges to no where... crossing over into the future to get back to us... In a world of controversy.... purple weeps... as the heavens declare our love... the rain has ended... the passion lives on... the nocturnal angel... cries herself to sleep.

Erupted into Words

I kept on going deep
and deeper,

Until

I disappeared and erupted
into words.

The Soul of a Goddess

You have captured me with both your beauty and your words. I have been entangled in a beautiful fantasy and world of wonderment. I am so blessed you have allowed me time to see and feel what you hold within. While others are and were attracted to what they saw, your poetry projects your hearts feelings from your soul which I felt more than what I saw. It was then that I saw your total beauty…and the more I read your words, the more I see into your soul…the soul of a Goddess.

It has been a beautiful journey,
Love always, Goddess

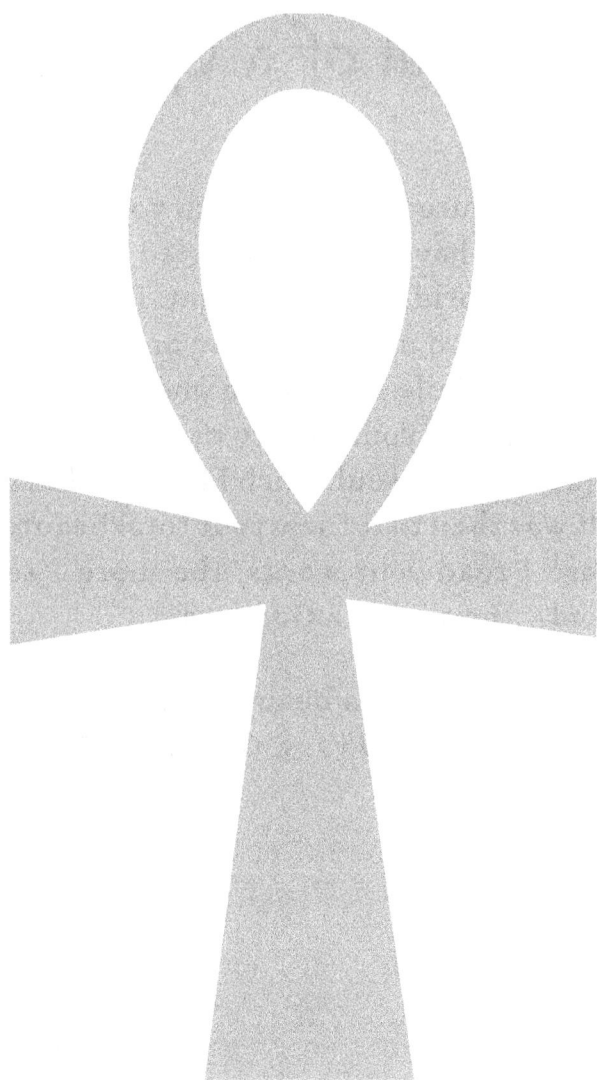

Acknowledgments

I would like to give a special thanks to my publisher, fellow poets and mentors for all their support and inspiration: Alice Maldonado Gallardo, BethAnne Kapansky Wright, Carolyn Riker, Michelle Reid, Catherine Schweig, Maureen Kwiat Meshenberg, Trina Shur, Andre Henderson, Ezzard Donahue, Douglas Davis, Richard Briggs, Dudley Paul, Angel Ross Garmon, Jyo Jyotirmoy, Stan Hill, Weston Weigand, Mary Trimble, Marcia Cheathem, Tasha Roberts, Julius Howard, Sheila Rhodes, Ezra Blackwell, William Purnell, Lindsey Rhodes, Vincent Alexander, Vladimir Petrosanec, Joseph M. Goodman, Shonda Henderson, Alex Harper, Kenneth Carroll, Sarada Kali Djedi, Tony Lodato II, Jasmin Peart, Clayton Homes, Tracy Beh, and many more…

About the Author

Sonja is a rising poetess, a free spirit, dreamer and spiritualist. She was born in Chicago and now resides in Texas with her husband and three beautiful daughters. Although, she fell in love with words at a very young age, she didn't become interested in writing poetry until after winning a poetry recital contest in high school. Sonja holds a B.A. in Spanish though her life's passion is poetry.

She has an unusual style of poetry, mystical, passionate, otherworldly. Her words are divinely inspired. She hopes to inspire women all around the globe to awaken to the inner goddess.

Sonja is author of *Living Poetry: Perceptions of a Goddess*. Several of her poems were published in the anthology *Where Journeys Meet: The Voice of Women's Poetry* and some of her poems will be published in two forthcoming anthologies.

www.facebook.com/sonjap3

www.facebook.com/Sonnets-and-Poems-of-a-Goddess

Author's Published Works

Book:

Living Poetry: Perceptions of a Goddess

The following poems were published in the anthology *Where Journeys Meet: The Voice of Women's Poetry* edited by Catherine Ghosh:

Awaken to the Sun
The Covenant Within
Inner Mystery
The Winter of my Undoing

Poems to be published in the forthcoming anthology *Hidden Lights: A Collection of Truths Not Often Told* edited by BethAnne Kapansky Wright & Carolyn Riker:

Unveiling the Mystery
Ancient Hymns of Her
Inner Poet
When the Angels Fly
Away, I Fly

Poems to be published in the forthcoming anthology *GODDESS: When She Rules: Expressions by Contemporary Women* edited by Catherine Schweig:

Ancient Hymns of Her
Inner Poet

www.ingramcontent.com/pod-product-compliance
Lightning Source LLC
Chambersburg PA
CBHW060242050426
42448CB00009B/1555